50 THINGS YOU SHOULD KNOW ABOUT THE CIVIL WAR

John D. Wright

Design and Editorial: Tall Tree Ltd
Consultant: Dr. Susannah J. Ural

Copyright © QEB Publishing, Inc. 2017

Published in the United States by
QEB Publishing, Inc.
Part of the Quarto Group
6 Orchard
Lake Forest, CA 92630

A CIP record for this book is available
from the Library of Congress.

ISBN 978 1 68297 157 4

Printed in China

Words in **bold** are explained
in the glossary on page 78.

CONTENTS

INTRODUCTION

▼ *The United States Capitol during the swearing in of President Lincoln on March 4, 1861. Lincoln's win triggered the breakaway of the Southern states.*

The United States was 84 years old when it began to fall apart. One reason was that the Northern and Southern parts of the country were very different. Eventually, arguments about slavery split the country. The proslave South formed itself into the **Confederacy** and the North remained the **Union**. Fighting soon broke out, and from 1861 to 1865, civil war raged in the U.S.

WHO WAS INVOLVED?

Some remarkable men and women were drawn into the war. Among them were the brilliant military men Ulysses S. Grant and Robert E. Lee, great political minds like Abraham Lincoln, journalists such as Horace Greeley, and brave slaves such as Harriet Tubman. Louisa May Alcott, author of *Little Women*, was a Union nurse, as was the poet Walt Whitman. Writer Mark Twain joined the Confederate volunteers. The war also attracted outlaws such as Frank and Jesse James, who fought for the Confederacy.

▲ *Author Mark Twain served in the Confederate army for just two weeks at the start of the war.*

COULD THE SOUTH WIN?

The two sides were not equal. The North had a large population and booming factories. The South had neither, and very few Southerners actually owned slaves. Its leaders believed the North would not risk lives and money to keep the Union together. They believed that, if a war started, Southerners could defend their land until the North got tired of fighting. If the war carried on, they expected Britain to support the South against the United States, Britain's former enemy.

UNION STATES

CONFEDERATE STATES

▲ Slaves working in the sweet potato fields of the Hopkinson Plantation, South Carolina, 1862.

▼ At Missionary Ridge, Tennessee, on November 25, 1863, Major General Ulysses S. Grant defeated the Confederate Army led by General Braxton Bragg. Casualties on both sides were heavy.

A FOUR-YEAR WAR

Many on both sides thought the war would be over within a few months. General Grant said: "*I, as well as thousands of other citizens, believed that the rebellion would collapse suddenly and soon if a decisive victory could be gained.*" However, no sudden victory happened, and the war dragged on for four years.

A country divided

Written in 1776, the Declaration of Independence stated that "All men are created equal." However, many people saw slaves as property, not equal men. The Founding Fathers, who led the American Revolution, were troubled by slavery, even though some of them owned slaves. When the Northern states abolished slavery in 1804 and the Southern states refused, the country was divided.

▶ *Signing of the Declaration of Independence, July 4, 1776.*

▲ *A slave trader takes bids during the auction of a slave.*

WHO BROUGHT THE SLAVES?

The British began shipping slaves to their American **colonies** (British settlements) in the 1660s. Slave traders in Boston and other ports became the main suppliers, shipping captured men and women in wretched conditions from West Africa. About 15 percent of the slaves died during the voyage.

Thomas Jefferson, who wrote the Declaration of Independence, owned 600 slaves.

KEY EVENTS

★ **July 4, 1776**
Declaration of Independence is signed, but does not address the problem of slavery (see above).

★ **January 1, 1808**
The United States makes it illegal to import slaves, but slave numbers in the South still increase (see page 7).

★ **1840s onward**
Waves of immigration to the Northern states create booming cities with factories (see page 9).

★ **May 30, 1854**
The Kansas–Nebraska Act allows those two territories to decide if they want slavery (see page 8).

SLAVERY BANNED

In 1808, the United States made it illegal to import slaves to any part of the country. However, it allowed the trading of slaves in slave states. Slaves continued to have babies, which increased the slave population naturally. By 1860, the year before the war began, slave numbers in the Southern states reached around 4 million.

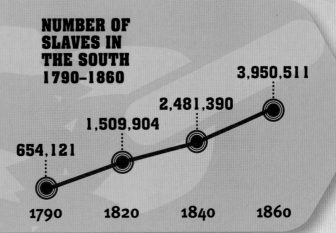

NUMBER OF SLAVES IN THE SOUTH 1790–1860

654,121 — 1790
1,509,904 — 1820
2,481,390 — 1840
3,950,511 — 1860

▲ African-American slaves separate cotton fibers using a cotton gin.

NAT TURNER

In 1830, a Virginia slave named Nat Turner killed his master and his master's family as they slept. Joined by about 60 more slaves, Turner and his band roamed the countryside and murdered another 55 people. A **militia** put an end to the revolt. After a trial, Turner and 16 others were hanged, and local whites killed up to 200 slaves in revenge. Southerners blamed the **abolitionists** for the revolt.

▲ The discovery and capture of Nat Turner.

WHY ONLY THE SOUTH?

As it expanded, the young United States developed two different economies. The North accepted a large number of immigrants, and this created a rapid growth in industry and business in its larger cities. The South's prosperity came from agriculture, especially cotton. Production boomed after Eli Whitney invented the cotton gin (a machine that separates fibers from seeds). The large **plantations** needed a large workforce, and filled it with slaves.

March 6, 1857
Dred Scott, a slave, asks for his freedom in 1857. The courts rule he has no legal rights (see page 10).

December 2, 1859
John Brown, a radical abolitionist, is hanged for trying to start a slave rebellion (see page 11).

November 6, 1860
Abraham Lincoln, an abolitionist, is elected President of the United States (see page 12).

February 1, 1861
Texas is the seventh Southern state to leave the Union and join the Confederacy (see page 13).

A divided Congress

2

Congress struggled to agree over the issue of slavery. In 1820, the U.S. had 11 slave states and 11 free states. The lawyer Henry Clay convinced Congress to admit the new territory of Missouri as a slave state and have Maine as a free state, to keep the balance. Maine was admitted in 1820.

▲ Henry Clay represented Kentucky in the House of Representatives and the Senate.

KEY

Free states

Slave states

Slavery decided by territories

0   300 miles

0   200 400 kilometers

▲ In the Kansas–Nebraska Act of 1854, slavery was decided by popular vote at state level.

NEW COMPROMISES

As more territories were added, the problem of what to do about slavery grew. This led to the Compromise of 1850. California would be admitted as a free state, while slavery in the District of Columbia, home to Washington, the nation's capital, would be banned. Next came the Kansas–Nebraska Act of 1854. This allowed those two territories to decide if they wanted slavery.

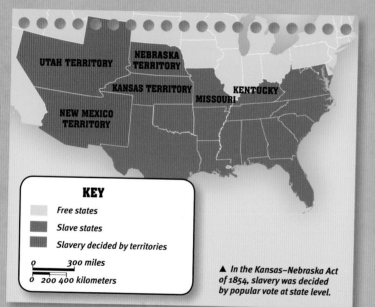

▼ Preston Brooks (second from the right), attacks abolitionist Charles Sumner.

CHARLES SUMNER

Charles Sumner, a senator from Massachusetts, opposed slavery. When he made an insulting speech about the Kansas–Nebraska Act, revenge was taken. On May 22, 1856, Preston Brooks, nephew of the Act's co-author, approached Sumner at his desk in the Senate and beat him unconscious with a cane.

Immigration and industrialization

There are two major reasons why the North became more powerful: immigrants chose to live in the North rather than the South, and the North's cities had more industry. By 1860, the 23 Northern states had a population of 21 million, while the 11 Southern states had 9 million, of whom 4 million were slaves. The North had 100,000 factories with 1.1 million workers, and the South had 20,000 factories and 100,000 workers.

▼ The piers and wharfs of the Wall Street Ferry in New York City—the first view of America for many arriving immigrants.

WHY SETTLE IN THE NORTH?

It was easier for immigrants to travel to the North because shipping routes tended to end in the North's ports. Fewer immigrants chose the South, since slavery had taken away many jobs. The North also had a larger mix of immigrants. Germans and Irish had their own units during the war. Several regiments were composed of Germans who spoke German on the battlefield.

▲ By 1860, the Tredegar Iron Works in Richmond was one of the largest iron manufacturers in the country.

ARMING THE SOUTH

With almost no heavy industry, the Confederacy desperately turned to the Tredegar Iron Works in Richmond, Virginia. Despite shortages in raw materials and trained workers, it manufactured more than 1,000 cannons and the plates needed for ironclad ships.

Dred Scott

Born a slave in Virginia, Dred Scott was bought by Dr. John Emerson, a surgeon. Dr. Emerson moved frequently, taking Scott with him. After eight years of living in Illinois and Wisconsin, both nonslave areas, Dr. Emerson died and Scott asked for his freedom. Scott argued that his time living in nonslave areas had made him free. His case went to the U.S. Supreme Court. In 1857, it ruled that Scott had no legal rights, as he was not a citizen.

▲ *This photograph of Dred Scott was taken after the Supreme Court verdict, in 1857.*

WHAT HAPPENED NEXT?

The sons of Scott's first owner, Peter Blow, were so upset by the court's decision that they paid Scott's legal fees, bought Scott and his wife, and in 1857 set them free. Scott was hired as a porter in a St. Louis hotel but died after only nine months of freedom.

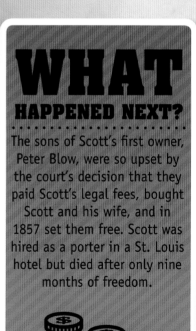

A BROADER RULING

The Supreme Court judges in Scott's case ruled that Congress had no right to free slaves in the western territories. They said that the 1820 Missouri Compromise (see page 8) that banned slavery there was unconstitutional because slaves were property, and their owners should be allowed to take them anywhere, including to nonslave territories. This ruling turned many people in the North against slavery.

John Brown

In 1856, a radical abolitionist named John Brown was living in Lawrence in the Kansas territory when the town was raided by proslavery men. Brown and his sons attacked and killed five of them. On October 16, 1859, Brown led 21 men to raid the federal armory at Harpers Ferry, Virginia, hoping to start a slave rebellion.

◀ John Brown pictured in the 1850s.

ARMORY ATTACK

Brown took several local people hostage in the armory. Arriving to put down the raid was a company of U.S. Marines led by Colonel Robert E. Lee, who would lead Confederate forces less than two years later. The marines stormed the armory, captured Brown, and killed 10 men, including two of Brown's sons. Brown was tried and hanged with six other men who had helped him.

BROWN'S LEGACY

During the war, Union soldiers marched to the inspirational song, "John Brown's Body," which would be rewritten as "The Battle Hymn of the Republic" (see page 42). One popular version began:

> John Brown's body lies
> a-moldering in the grave;
> John Brown's body lies
> a-moldering in the grave;
> John Brown's body lies
> a-moldering in the grave;
>
> His soul's marching on.
> Glory, halle—hallelujah!
> Glory, halle—hallelujah!
> Glory, halle—hallelujah!
> His soul's marching on!

John Brown raided the Harpers Ferry armory to steal weapons for his rebellion.

▲ Brown (center, holding a rifle) stands over his hostages at the Harpers Ferry Armory, just as U.S. Marines are breaking in.

As well as opposing slavery, Lincoln was strongly in favor of women having the vote.

Abraham Lincoln elected

▶ *The first photograph of Lincoln as President, 1861.*

After years working in menial jobs, Abraham Lincoln taught himself law and became a successful lawyer in Illinois. He served two years in the U.S. House of Representatives, where he was known for his views against slavery, which he called "a moral, social, and political evil." Impressed by his honesty and vision, the Republican Party nominated him in 1860 and he was elected the nation's 16th President that year.

WHY WAS THE SOUTH WORRIED?

Although Lincoln was against slavery, he said that he did not want to interfere with it in states where it existed. "I believe I have no lawful right to do so," he said, "and I have no inclination to do so." Southerners, however, did not trust his words and were worried about his determination not to allow any states to leave the Union. By the time he was inaugurated on March 4, 1861, seven states had **seceded** and formed the Confederacy.

▲ *Stephen A. Douglas, the Democratic nominee in the 1860 election, opposed slavery, and split the Democratic Party.*

The Southern states secede

Southern states wanted to leave the Union before Lincoln took power. South Carolina led the way and after six more states followed, the government of the Confederacy was set up in Montgomery, Alabama, on February 4, 1861. It elected Jefferson Davis, a Mississippi senator, as President.

◀ *Jefferson Davis was a former soldier, born on a cotton plantation.*

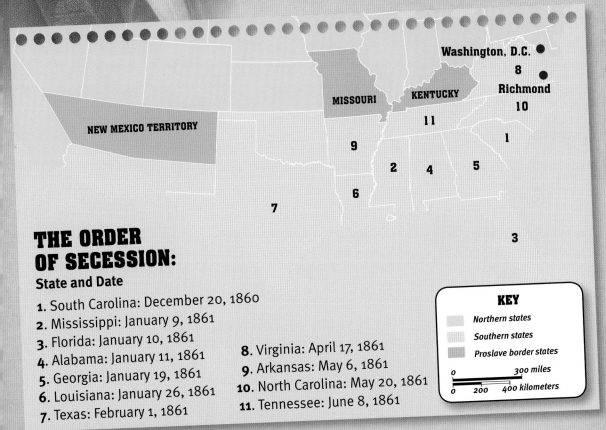

THE ORDER OF SECESSION:

State and Date

1. South Carolina: December 20, 1860
2. Mississippi: January 9, 1861
3. Florida: January 10, 1861
4. Alabama: January 11, 1861
5. Georgia: January 19, 1861
6. Louisiana: January 26, 1861
7. Texas: February 1, 1861
8. Virginia: April 17, 1861
9. Arkansas: May 6, 1861
10. North Carolina: May 20, 1861
11. Tennessee: June 8, 1861

KEY

Northern states
Southern states
Proslave border states

0   300 miles
0   200   400 kilometers

RELUCTANT REBELS

Many Southerners were unhappy about seceding from the country they had belonged to all their lives. A series of state conventions was held to discuss the matter and vote on secession. Pockets of U.S. supporters, especially in Alabama and Tennessee, resisted the Confederacy during the war and supplied soldiers to the Union army.

1861–1862

The war begins

There was always the possibility that the South might successfully secede without a war. Confederate President Jefferson Davis often said, "All we ask is to be left alone." President Lincoln, however, was determined to preserve the United States. He allowed Confederate states to take over some U.S. forts, but he refused to hand over Fort Sumter in South Carolina.

▼ Confederate soldiers fire cannons at Fort Sumter, which was located on an island off Charleston, South Carolina.

KEY EVENTS

April 14, 1861
Confederate guns fire at the Union's Fort Sumter, starting the U.S. Civil War (see above).

July 21, 1861
Heavy fighting takes place at the Battle of Bull Run. The Confederates secure a victory (see page 17).

October 21, 1861
Union forces suffer another embarrassing defeat at Ball's Bluff in Virginia. (see page 18).

April 7, 1862
Both sides are battered at the Battle of Shiloh, which the Union army eventually wins (see page 20).

THE FIRST SHOTS

Fort Sumter was low on supplies but its commander, Major Robert Anderson, refused to leave. On April 14, 1861, Confederate guns led by General Beauregard bombarded the fort. Anderson returned fire for 34 hours, but surrendered the next day. The war had now started. The next day, Lincoln called for 75,000 men to put down the uprising.

WHAT ABOUT SLAVERY?

Both sides insisted the war was not about slavery. Jefferson Davis said: "We are not fighting for slavery. We are fighting for independence." Even Lincoln said in his inaugural speech: "I have no purpose, directly or indirectly, to interfere with the institution of slavery in the states where it exists." Congress also passed a resolution in 1861 saying that the war's aim was to reunite the country, and this kept the slave-holding border states of Maryland, Delaware, Kentucky, and Missouri in the Union.

MAJOR ROBERT ANDERSON

Fort Sumter's commander was born in Kentucky and once owned slaves. After he evacuated the fort, Lincoln promoted him to brigadier general and the North hailed him as "the hero of Fort Sumter." When the Union recaptured Fort Sumter in 1865, Anderson returned to raise its original flag.

◄ *Major Robert Anderson, who first refused to leave Fort Sumter.*

GENERAL BEAUREGARD

Pierre Beauregard was born on his family's sugarcane plantation near New Orleans, Louisiana. He was the Confederacy's first brigadier general and designed their famous battle flag (see page 74). He oversaw the bombardment of Fort Sumter.

◄ *General Pierre Gustave Toutant Beauregard.*

April 12, 1862
Union soldiers try to cripple the South's rail network by stealing a Confederate locomotive (see page 25).

May 31, 1862
Thaddeus Lowe observes the enemy from a balloon at the Battle of Fairs Oaks in Virginia (see page 24).

September 15, 1862
Confederates invade Maryland and thousands are killed in the Battle of Antietam (see page 21).

June 2, 1863
Former slave Harriet Tubman helps around 756 slaves to escape in South Carolina (see page 22).

Grant and Lee

Although their armies fought each other for four years, Union general Ulysses S. Grant and Confederate general Robert E. Lee had a lot in common. Both graduated from the military academy West Point, and they fought together in the Mexican War of 1846–1848. Both owned slaves and freed them. When the war began, they were both asked to command the U.S. Army.

GENERAL GRANT

Born Hiram Ulysses Grant in Ohio, Grant became a brigadier general in the war's first year. He won fame in 1862 by capturing 15,000 Confederate troops at Fort Donelson, Tennessee. Grant won many victories, including at Vicksburg (see page 35) and Chattanooga, before being made general-in-chief of all Union armies in March 1864. His nine-month siege of General Lee's men at Petersburg led to the end of the war.

◄ *Portrait of General Robert E. Lee, 1863.*

◄ *Portrait of General Ulysses S. Grant, 1867.*

GENERAL LEE

At the outbreak of war, Virginia-born Robert E. Lee turned down an offer to lead the Union armies. In 1862, he took command of the Army of Northern Virginia. He won great victories at Fredericksburg and Chancellorsville, but his mistakes lost Gettysburg. By February 1865, Lee was in command of all Confederate forces, but he surrendered two months later.

Battle of Bull Run

Bull Run, called the Battle of Manassas by the South, took place on July 21, 1861. Union troops under General Irvin McDowell were sent to drive the Confederates of General Beauregard from the railroad junction at Manassas, Virginia. Confederate reinforcements under General "Stonewall" Jackson arrived by train. The battle was fought between 37,000 Union soldiers and 32,232 Confederates.

▼ The Rebel cavalry attacks at the First Battle of Bull Run, July 21, 1861.

WHAT HAPPENED NEXT?

During heavy fighting, General Jackson got his nickname "Stonewall" for standing firm under fire. Beauregard's men advanced and Union forces fled in panic. McDowell's battle plan was too complex for inexperienced Union troops. The Confederates were able to bring in reinforcements just as Union soldiers became exhausted. The battle was a great victory for the South. Total casualties were 2,645 for the Union and 1,981 for the Confederacy.

▲ General Stonewall Jackson monitors the action of the Battle at Bull Run, Virginia, in July 1861.

ANOTHER BATTLE

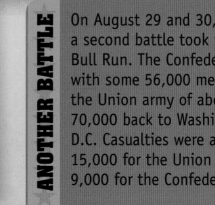

On August 29 and 30, 1862, a second battle took place at Bull Run. The Confederates, with some 56,000 men, drove the Union army of about 70,000 back to Washington, D.C. Casualties were about 15,000 for the Union and 9,000 for the Confederacy.

Washington's elite brought picnics to watch the battle, but were horrified by the violence.

Battle of Ball's Bluff

Union forces were defeated again at Ball's Bluff, Virginia, on October 21, 1861. Colonel Edward Baker, a U.S. senator, led his men to reinforce Union soldiers facing the enemy across the Potomac River. The Confederates were led by General Nathan Evans. The Union lost 48 men, including Baker, the only senator killed in battle during the war.

▲ Colonel Edward D. Baker at the war's outbreak in 1861.

WHAT WENT WRONG?

Baker decided to cross the river with only four small boats available, which slowed his attack. After he was killed by gunfire, his men became trapped on the riverbank, where the smaller Confederate force easily shot them down. Some drowned in the river trying to escape.

▼ Colonel Baker is killed by a bullet through his heart at Ball's Bluff, near Leesburg, Virginia, on October 21, 1861.

WHY DID LINCOLN WEEP?

Colonel Baker was a longtime personal friend of President Lincoln, who had named his second son after him: Edward Baker Lincoln. Baker rode with Lincoln to his inauguration and introduced him to the crowd. When told of Baker's death, Lincoln was deeply upset and was seen crying.

AFTER THE DEFEAT

The embarrassing defeat at Ball's Bluff led to Congress establishing the Joint Committee on the Conduct of the War. Led by Radical Republicans, it investigated battle defeats, the loyalty and ability of officers, and many other issues.

Bodies were floating downriver to Washington, D.C. for days after Ball's Bluff.

The telegraph

The U.S. Military Telegraph Corps supported the Union army. They laid a network of **telegraph** lines nicknamed "the grapevine" and sent messages from special wagons. General Grant could keep in constant contact with his armies and with Lincoln. Union generals sometimes tapped into enemy wires to learn the Confederacy's plans.

▼ *War reporters sit together in a Union army camp. Battle reports were sent by telegraph from wagons like the* New York Herald Tribune *one on the right.*

THE CONFEDERATE ANSWER

When the war began, the Union had a big advantage over the South's smaller telegraph networks. The Southern Telegraph Company, the largest in the Confederacy, was reluctant to give its full support to the war. Eventually it had to be placed under military control.

BREAKING CODES

Since most important messages were sent in code, both sides had specialist code-breakers. One of the best was a Confederate private, Charles A. Gaston, serving under General Lee. He once hid for six weeks in the Virginia woods near General Grant's headquarters reading Grant's coded messages. When Confederate agents failed to decrypt codes, some were published in Southern newspapers with a reward offered for solving them.

▲ *The Military Telegraph Corps is seen here laying wires, known as "the grapevine." The equipment is housed in the wagon.*

Hitting back

By 1862, the opposing armies were becoming more equal as both sides gained experience. Union armies were hitting back with more force. Confederate armies relied on brilliant tactics to mislead and surprise the enemy.

BATTLE OF SHILOH

On April 6, 1862, General Grant's army was camped near Pittsburg Landing on the Tennessee River when it was attacked by Confederates under General Albert Sidney Johnston. Intense **artillery** fighting was followed by fierce combat at a peach orchard, where Johnston was killed. General Beauregard replaced him. The Confederates had captured 2,200 enemy troops but were running out of ammunition. Union gunboats pounded them and that evening further Union reinforcements arrived. The Union won the battle on the second day. Beauregard withdrew, but Grant's troops were too battered to pursue.

HALTING THE ADVANCE

Three horrific battles in 1862 made it clear that the war would be long and bloody. The Battle of Shiloh proved such a costly win for the Union that the Confederates also claimed victory. The Battle of Antietam, which saw more deaths than any other battle in the war, stopped General Lee's advance but was not a total Union victory. Fredericksburg was a defensive fight for the Confederates.

▼ *Union troops form a line of heavy artillery fire at the Battle of Shiloh, April 1862.*

At the Battle of Shiloh, the Union lost 13,047 men, the Confederates 10,699.

◀ Battle sites of Shiloh, Antietam, and Fredericksburg.

BATTLE OF ANTIETAM

Also called Sharpsburg, this battle became the bloodiest day of the war. General Lee invaded Maryland with 40,000 men. On September 15, they took positions on a ridge, facing about 95,000 Union men under General McClellan. Two days later the battle began. At one point the opposing armies surged back and forth over a cornfield where about 8,000 men fell. Fierce fighting occurred at a sunken road later called "the Bloody Lane." On one day, the Union suffered 12,401 casualties and the Confederacy 10,318.

▲ The 51st New York Infantry and 51st Pennsylvania Infantry cross Burnside's Bridge in the thick of the Battle of Antietam, September 17, 1862.

BATTLE OF FREDERICKSBURG

General Lee's forces were occupying the heights around Fredericksburg, Virginia, and Union General Ambrose Burnside was determined to remove them. On December 13, 1862, his men crossed the Rappahannock River. It proved to be a suicidal mission. By the afternoon, the Union army had to retreat. Union casualties were 13,000, compared to 5,300 on the Confederate side, and two generals were killed.

▲ Union soldiers use pontoon bridges to cross the Rappahannock River before they attack Fredericksburg on December 13, 1862.

Harriet Tubman

◀ An 1863 portrait of Tubman. Although illiterate, she was a powerful abolitionist speaker.

Araminta Ross was born a slave in Maryland. Married to a free black, John Tubman, she escaped in 1849 when she thought that her children might be sold. Changing her first name to Harriet, she began risking her life to help hundreds of slaves escape along the Underground Railroad, a network of slave escape routes and safe houses.

HELPING JOHN BROWN

When the abolitionist John Brown was planning his attack on the **armory** at Harpers Ferry in 1859 (see page 11), Tubman met with him in Canada to give him details about that area of Virginia. Brown nicknamed her "General Tubman" and called her "one of the best and bravest persons on this continent."

▼ *Escaped slaves passing along a route of the Underground Railroad.*

LEADING SOLDIERS

Tubman acted as a spy and a scout during the war. On June 2, 1863, she led Union soldiers up the Combahee River in South Carolina to free some 756 slaves. She helped General David Hunter, who formed the 1st South Carolina Volunteers, an African-American Union regiment, serving as his nurse and cook. She also worked alongside Clara Barton, founder of the American Red Cross (see page 53).

Tubman traveled 19 times to the South to rescue slaves, despite a bounty for her capture.

Medical advances

Soldiers sometimes faced as much horror in field hospitals as they did in battle. Conditions were basic, and there were often no medicines, especially in the South. **Anesthetic** was not always available, even for limb **amputations**. Nothing was known about germs and **penicillin**, and instruments were not disinfected. However, as the war went on, medical treatment got better.

▲ An amputation being performed in a hospital tent at Gettysburg, July 1863.

▲ Nurses and officers of the U.S. Sanitary Commission, photographed at Fredericksburg, Virginia, in the winter of 1862.

DOROTHEA DIX

As the war began, a 59-year-old mental health activist named Dorothea Dix became superintendent of the Union's female nurses. Unpaid, she recruited nurses, worked with Clara Barton to develop a professional service, improved medical care, and set up and inspected hospitals. Only 5 feet tall, she was known as "Dragon Dix" for her bossy nature.

WHAT CHANGED?

During the war, both sides' armies built new "pavilion" (single-story) hospitals. Doctors learned new operating methods, proper medical records were kept, nursing became professional, and ambulance crews were trained. Northern care was better, helped by more than 3,000 nurses and the civilian United States Sanitary Commission, which introduced strict hygiene. First aid and anesthetics began to arrive on the battlefield to treat the wounded before they were taken to the hospital. In general, the medical services of both sides became more orderly and efficient.

At Fredericksburg, the Union had only 40 surgeons to treat 7,000 wounded men.

Up in the air

The Union's balloon Intrepid had a portrait of General McClellan's face on its side.

▼ A ground crew lets go of the ropes as Thaddeus Lowe ascends in the basket of the Intrepid, in 1862.

President Lincoln set up the Balloon Corps and appointed Thaddeus Lowe as chief of Army Aeronautics. Lowe was given seven balloons to observe the enemy. Two **hydrogen** generators were used to inflate them. Lowe carried a camera to photograph enemy positions and a telegraph key to send messages about where to direct artillery fire.

WAS USING A BALLOON DANGEROUS?

The enemy often fired artillery shells at the balloon. If in danger, the balloonist could pull a control valve to release gas and descend. General Fitz-John Porter once drifted behind Confederate lines before he was luckily blown back toward his camp. After that, General McClellan wrote, "You won't catch me in the confounded balloon nor will I allow any other generals to go up in it."

▼ A balloon is inflated to observe the Battle of Fair Oaks, May 1862.

HOW REBELS TRICKED LOWE

Lowe observed the enemy during the Peninsula Campaign, a major Union operation in Virginia in 1862. He ascended to some 1,000 feet and was spotted by the Confederates. They then marched out of the woods and circled back into the trees several times. This made it look as if they were a much larger force, a deception that helped stop the Union's advance.

Railroads

The easiest way to move troops and equipment was by rail, and railroads played a major role in the war. The Union had the most tracks by far: 22,000 miles. The South had 9,500 miles. The Confederacy relied on the railroad as it had fewer troops and needed to transport men quickly from one battle to another.

▲ The General, *before its theft by Union forces in 1862.*

THE GREAT CHASE

On April 12, 1862, 18 Union soldiers, led by the spy James Andrews, stole *The General*, a Confederate locomotive. Their aim was to cripple the South's rail network. The locomotive's engineer, William Fuller, chased them on foot, by **handcar**, and finally in another locomotive. After seven hours and 87 miles, *The General* ran out of fuel. Andrews and seven others were hanged. Nineteen raiders became the first soldiers to be awarded the **Medal of Honor**.

◀ *Soldiers with a mortar on a small railroad car.*

▲ *General Sherman's men destroy the railroad as they march through Georgia in 1864.*

SHERMAN'S NECKTIES

One tactic of the Union army was to destroy railroads so that the enemy could not use them (see pages 40–41). General Sherman caused the worst damage in the South. His men pulled up tracks, heated them until they were red-hot, and then bent them around trees, sometimes twisting them into a circle. The results were nicknamed "Sherman's neckties" and "Sherman's hairpins."

The South's railroads were fragile, designed to transport cotton, not heavy artillery.

1863–1864

The Union strikes back

President Lincoln wanted to address the central issue that was dividing the nation, the issue of slavery. In July 1862, he read to his **cabinet** the draft of his Emancipation Proclamation to free the slaves. When the Union's military fortunes improved after victory at Antietam in September, Lincoln publicly issued his historic decree.

◀ *The Emancipation Proclamation took effect on January 1, 1863.*

▼ *Abraham Lincoln reads the Emancipation Proclamation to his cabinet on July 22, 1862. William Henry Seward sits opposite him.*

KEY EVENTS

★ **March 9, 1862**
The ironclad ships *Monitor* and *Merrimack* clash, causing little damage (see pages 38–39).

★ **January 1, 1863**
The Emancipation Proclamation, aimed at freeing the slaves, takes effect (see above).

★ **June 27, 1863**
The Union wins at Gettysburg, where Lincoln gives his famous address (see pages 32–34).

★ **July 4, 1863**
The Confederates surrender at Vicksburg, Mississippi, after a 40-day siege (see page 35).

▼ *Columbia, female symbol of America, holds the Declaration of Emancipation between two slaves draped in the U.S. flag of 1863.*

WHAT EFFECT DID IT HAVE?

In real terms, the Emancipation Proclamation freed no slaves. It announced their freedom in any state or part of a state whose people were in rebellion against the United States. Emancipation was practically impossible, since the Union had no control over Confederate states. In addition, the proclamation did not free slaves in the Union's border states. Its true effect was to change the reason for the war from maintaining the union to freeing the slaves. This won great approval in Britain, which had abolished slavery.

▼ *William Henry Seward, pictured during the war.*

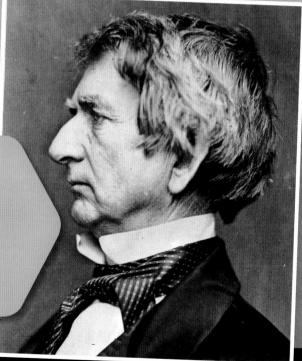

SECRETARY OF STATE

William Henry Seward was the U.S. Secretary of State from 1861 to 1869. He convinced Lincoln to delay issuing the Emancipation Proclamation until the Union's military fortunes had improved. Lincoln listened to him and issued the proclamation five days after the victory at the Battle of Antietam. The famous decree took effect on January 1, 1863.

July 18, 1863
The first African-American regiments see action at Fort Wagner, South Carolina (see page 36).

June 19, 1864
The Confederate ship the *Alabama* is sunk off the coast of France (see pages 38–39).

November 16, 1864
Union General Sherman begins his famous march through Georgia toward the sea (see pages 40–41).

April 26, 1864
Sherman accepts the surrender of Confederate General Johnston (see page 41).

General Stonewall Jackson

Thomas Jonathan Jackson was a brilliant Confederate leader. He was known for smart tactics and the rapid way he moved his troops, once covering 51 miles in two days. During 1862, he defeated three Union armies and took 13,000 prisoners at Harpers Ferry, the largest ever surrender of a Union force.

▶ General Stonewall Jackson in 1861.

WHY STONEWALL?

During the First Battle of Bull Run, Jackson's troops stood their ground against fierce attacks. General Barnard Bee told his men, "There is Jackson standing like a stone wall. Rally behind the Virginians!" The Confederate Congress soon called Jackson's men the "Stonewall Brigade," the only brigade allowed a nickname.

▼ Confederate officers race to help Jackson after he was shot by his own men during the Battle of Chancellorsville.

ECCENTRIC HABITS

Jackson was very religious. He never touched liquor or tobacco, or swore. Troops delighted in his eccentric behavior. This included sitting stiffly upright, which he believed kept his internal organs in line.

A SURPRISING DEATH

During the Battle of Chancellorsville on May 2, 1862, Jackson rode beyond his front line to observe the enemy. When returning, his own men mistook him for a Union soldier and shot him three times. He died eight days later.

General Jackson's finger was shot off during the First Battle of Bull Run.

General W. T. Sherman

William T. Sherman was called both a genius and a madman. He led a Union brigade in the First Battle of Bull Run and was wounded at Shiloh, but kept fighting. He later commanded three Union armies and won victories at Vicksburg (see page 35) and Chattanooga. He also led Union forces on the march to the sea (see page 40).

◄ *General William Tecumseh Sherman in 1864.*

▲ *Sherman observes the Battle of Chattanooga in 1863. His troops were sent in to help the besieged Union army.*

GRANT AND SHERMAN

Generals Grant and Sherman were especially close. In fact, when Grant decided to resign during the war in 1862, it was Sherman who talked him into remaining. Soon after, Sherman wrote, "Grant stood by me when I was crazy and I stood by him when he was drunk; and now we stand by each other always."

WAS HE INSANE?

Sherman, called "Uncle Billy" by his men, was known for pacing around the camp talking to himself and behaving oddly. His wife said he had a "morbid sense of anxiety." Sherman's nervousness worried the secretary of war, who sent him home for a rest. A headline in a Cincinnati newspaper read: "GENERAL SHERMAN INSANE." He may have been eccentric, but he was too thoughtful and smart to be insane.

Sherman's middle name was Tecumseh, after a Native American chief of the Shawnees.

Military arms

When the war began, both sides were armed with **muskets**. To fire them, they had to be loaded from the muzzle end of the barrel with a ramrod. Some muskets had spiral grooves inside the barrel, called **rifling**, which caused the bullet to spin and travel farther and more accurately. The war saw many improvements in firearms, and the Union army was helped by the lever-action repeating rifle. This could be loaded from the trigger end, making it faster to operate.

▼ Reenactors dressed in Union army uniforms fire blanks from replica Springfield rifles.

SPRINGFIELD RIFLE

Produced by the Springfield Armory in Massachusetts, this rifle was the standard infantry weapon for both sides, as the Confederates produced their own version.

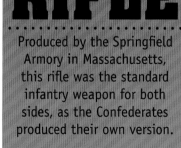

▲ U.S. Civil War Springfield Model 1861 rifle.

▼ Cartridges were stored in the butt of the Spencer rifle.

SPENCER REPEATING RIFLE

With the arrival of the breech-loaded repeating rifle, a soldier's life became easier and less dangerous. The Spencer had a tube at the gun's butt that held seven **cartridges**. After a shot was taken, a new cartridge moved into firing position when the gun was cocked. More advanced still was the Union's repeating Henry rifle. This provided 16 shots without loading. Confederates complained that a Union soldier could "load on Sunday and shoot for the rest of the week."

MACHINE GUNS

The best-known early machine gun was the Gatling Gun, which had six barrels rotating around a central spindle. Although it was tested during the war, the Gatling Gun was only approved by the Union army after the war ended. Two other strange-looking machine guns were used only occasionally. The Billinghurst-Requa Volley Gun had a row of 25 rifle barrels between the wheels of a carriage. The Union Repeating Gun, usually called the Ager Coffee Mill Gun, had an open hopper on top that the operator filled with cartridges. It was fired using a hand crank.

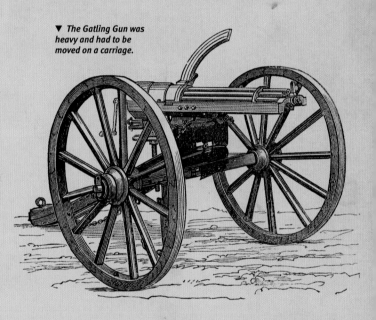

▼ The Gatling Gun was heavy and had to be moved on a carriage.

THE MINIÉ BALL

The Minié ball was a lead, cone-shaped bullet commonly used in the war. It had a hollow base that expanded when fired, making it more accurate. It was called the Minié ball after its French inventor and was first created by the French army in 1848. The large, soft bullet moved too slowly to pass quickly through a body and could cause terrible wounds.

◄ Wounds caused by Minié balls, such as these, were usually fatal.

Battle of Gettysburg

The war's most important battle was fought in the small town of Gettysburg in Pennsylvania. General Lee's army marched north into the state during June 1863. It was a risky move as the Confederates didn't know the area or how many Union troops were gathering under General Meade.

▼ The Union army charges toward the Confederates during the Battle of Gettysburg. The fighting was ferocious and thousands were killed.

STARTED BY SHOES?

It has been said that fighting broke out at Gettysburg because General Henry Heth had sent Confederate soldiers there in search of supplies. Shoes, in particular, were desperately needed. However, the Southern army probably went to Gettysburg simply because the road network in the area passed through the town.

◄ General Henry Heth

28,063 Confederate soldiers and 23,049 Union soldiers were killed at Gettysburg.

WHAT HAPPENED?

The battle on July 1 quickly grew. The Confederates attacked the Union troops and forced them back to Cemetery Ridge. The next day, the Union army occupied and held onto the ridge and two hills. During the third and last day of the battle, cannon fire from the Union army stopped. Lee ordered an attack over an open field, where Union soldiers gunned the Confederate soldiers down. As a result, the Confederates were defeated, but the Union leaders allowed them to retreat and get away.

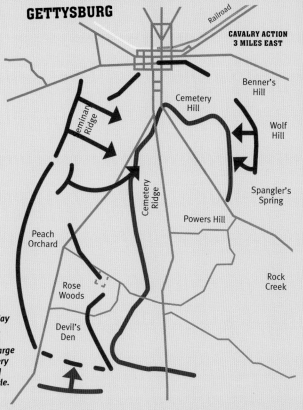

GETTYSBURG

Railroad

CAVALRY ACTION
3 MILES EAST

Benner's Hill

Cemetery Hill

Wolf Hill

Seminary Ridge

Cemetery Ridge

Spangler's Spring

Powers Hill

Peach Orchard

Rock Creek

Rose Woods

Devil's Den

▶ The last day of the battle, July 3, 1863. The fatal charge near Cemetery Ridge would end the battle.

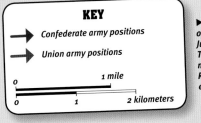

KEY

→ Confederate army positions

→ Union army positions

0		1 mile
0	1	2 kilometers

The disastrous charge at Gettysburg is known as "Pickett's Charge." General Lee ordered the attack, which was overseen by three generals, including General George Pickett. Even after it had failed, Lee wanted Pickett to charge again. Years later, Pickett blamed Lee for the massacre.

◀ General Pickett, who helped to lead the fatal charge.

WHY WAS LINCOLN DISAPPOINTED?

Despite the victory, President Lincoln was furious at General Meade for allowing Lee's forces to retreat. Lincoln said he was "deeply mortified by the escape of Lee" since he believed destroying his army would have ended the war.

▶ General George Meade won the Battle of Gettysburg but let the defeated Confederate army get away.

33

The Gettysburg Address

The Union wanted to remember the victory at Gettysburg, so they decided to turn the battlefield into a national military cemetery. At its dedication, on November 19, 1863, President Lincoln delivered his famous Gettysburg Address.

A GOOD SPEECH?

Today, the speech is seen as the greatest in U.S. history. Lincoln spoke about the principles of true equality and redefined the Civil War as a struggle to preserve the Union. His words were carefully chosen and made a huge impact. He, however, thought it was a failure, and would later say, "I failed, I failed, and that is about all that can be said about it."

▲ *Abraham Lincoln addresses the crowd at Gettysburg in November 1863.*

A SHOCKED AUDIENCE

Edward Everett gave the opening speech that lasted two hours. Lincoln then spoke for less than three minutes, leaving his audience surprised and disappointed. The speech was so short, no photographer was able to record it.

▶ *The former U.S. Secretary of State Edward Everett.*

LINCOLN'S WORDS

"Four score and seven years ago our fathers brought forth on this continent, a new nation, conceived in Liberty, and dedicated to the proposition that all men are created equal... It is rather for us to be here dedicated to the great task remaining before us... that we here highly resolve that these dead shall not have died in vain—that this nation, under God, shall have a new birth of freedom—and that government of the people, by the people, for the people, shall not perish from the earth."

Siege of Vicksburg

▲ *A Confederate cannon at Vicksburg. The gun was responsible for sinking the Union gunboat USS Cincinnati during the siege.*

The Confederacy used the Mississippi River to move supplies and they closely guarded the river from the city of Vicksburg. On May 18, 1863, General Grant besieged the city. This lasted 40 days until the Confederacy surrendered on July 4, 1863.

During the Vicksburg siege, many people had to hide in caves, which you can still visit.

▲ *Union soldiers under the command of General Grant besiege the city of Vicksburg, with the Mississippi River to the right.*

HARDSHIP HUMOR

Starving people trapped in the siege were forced to eat rats, dogs, horses, and mules. The *Chicago Tribune* printed an imaginary menu for the trapped people that included "Mule Tail Soup" and "Mule tongue cold a-la-Bray."

WHY DID GRANT SET THE ENEMY FREE?

One of the agreements Grant made with the Confederate General John Pemberton was to allow Pemberton's 31,000 men to march out free as long as they promised not to fight in the war again. Transporting so many men north would have been difficult. Many of the Confederate troops did, of course, rejoin the war.

African-American soldiers

In July 1862, Congress allowed African Americans to fight. Almost 200,000 served in Union armies and about 37,000 were killed. Their first regiment, formed in September 1862, was the Louisiana Native Guards, made up of 1,500 free blacks from Union-held New Orleans. The first regiment from the North was the 54th Massachusetts Volunteers, formed in January 1863.

HONORABLE FAILURE

The first big battle of the 54th Massachusetts was a failed attempt to take Fort Wagner in Charleston, South Carolina. They led the attack and suffered 272 casualties among their 600 soldiers. For his heroism during this action, Sergeant William H. Carney became the first African American to win the Congressional Medal of Honor.

▲ Two unidentified African-American soldiers in Union sergeant's uniforms, around 1863.

▼ African-American troops storm the walls of Fort Wagner on Morris Island, South Carolina, in July 1863.

FORT PILLOW MASSACRE

In April 1864, Confederates led by General Nathan Forrest attacked the Union's Fort Pillow in Tennessee. Union soldiers attempted to surrender but many, especially the African-American troops, were gunned down. Confederate soldiers often took revenge against former slaves and other African Americans fighting them.

Military technology

The Civil War was the first large conflict to use some of the hardware and tactics common in later warfare. These included motorized submarines to attack enemy shipping, land mines that were triggered by attacking troops, and new types of defensive positions that protected soldiers from heavy gunfire.

▼ *This Confederate torpedo boat was powered by eight men cranking a handle to turn the propeller.*

The Confederacy had 20 semi-submersible torpedo boats powered by steam engines.

LAND MINES

The Confederates introduced land mines. They attached friction primers (cylinders) to shells and buried them below ground to explode when stepped upon. These weapons were first found by Union soldiers on May 4, 1862, when they occupied Yorktown, Virginia.

DEFENSIVE POSITIONS

The Civil War saw the earliest uses of "rifle pits." A soldier lay down to fire from his hole or a trench, which was protected by a mound of earth in front. When laying siege to an enemy city, attacking troops dug a system of deep trenches to protect themselves from artillery and snipers.

▶ *Heavily fortified trenches at Petersburg, Virginia, 1863.*

Naval battles

When the war began, the Confederacy had only a few small ships to oppose the Union's large navy. The South fought back with hit-and-run tactics, the use of floating mines, and the first motorized submarines. It built an **ironclad** ship, the *Virginia*, which fought a famous battle with the ironclad *Monitor*. However, the South had little defense against a full attack by the North's fleet.

BATTLE OF THE IRONCLADS

The Civil War was the first time ironclads were used in battle. These were steam-powered warships protected by iron armor. Both sides raced to build ironclads. The Confederates covered a wooden **frigate** called the *Merrimack* with iron plates and renamed it the *Virginia*. The Union built the ironclad *Monitor*. They met at Hampton Roads, Virginia, on March 9, 1862, and the battle lasted three hours. Neither caused serious damage—shots simply bounced off the iron.

BLOCKADE

In April 1861, Lincoln announced the "Anaconda Plan," a blockade of Southern ports. The aim was to stop the South selling cotton overseas and to cut off its imports of arms, medicines, and food. The Confederacy tried to break this with blockade runners and privateers (licensed pirates), but the squeeze brought crippling hardships to their troops and civilians.

▼ *An illustration from 1861 showing Lincoln's Anaconda plan.*

▶ *The epic Battle of Hampton Roads raged for hours. Armor-piercing shells had not yet been invented, and neither ship caused much damage to the other.*

Britain's help for the South's navy almost led to war between Britain and the North.

THE *ALABAMA*

Britain built three ships for the Confederacy. The most famous, built in 1862, was the cruiser *Alabama*, which had many British sailors in its crew. Under the command of Raphael Semmes, it sailed the world attacking Union **merchant ships**. The *Alabama* captured 65 U.S. ships and burned 52 of them. It was sunk off France on June 19, 1864, by the *U.S.S. Kearsarge*, an ironclad disguised to look like a wooden frigate. Semmes and his crew were rescued by local boats.

▼ *The* U.S.S. Kearsarge *scores a direct hit on the Confederacy's* Alabama. *The* Alabama's *crew was rescued from the water and entertained in London before returning to the war.*

TIED TO THE MAST

On August 5, 1862, Union Admiral David Farragut sailed his fleet into Mobile Bay, Alabama, which was protected by mines known then as **torpedoes**. After seeing his leading ship, the ironclad *Tecumseh*, hit a mine and sink, Farragut had his men tie him to the mast of his ship where he shouted, "Damn the torpedoes! Full speed ahead!" Waiting for him was the Confederate *Tennessee*, the largest ironclad on either side in the war. After a three-hour battle, Farragut was victorious.

▲ *Admiral David Glasgow Farragut is tied to the mast of his ship, the* Hartford.

General Sherman's destruction of Georgia is known as "scorched earth" warfare.

28 Sherman's march to the sea

After taking Atlanta on September 2, 1864, General William T. Sherman was ready for the next stage in the war. He decided to march through Georgia to South Carolina. Along the way, he would feed his armies by taking what they found on the land. He said he wanted the South to suffer for starting the war and he vowed to "make Georgia howl."

WHAT HAPPENED?

Sherman began his famous march through Georgia on November 16. Around 62,000 men had to pass through 270 miles of enemy territory. The Confederates, led by General Joseph E. Johnston, were weak and unable to stop Sherman's powerful army. The Union army arrived and took the port of Savannah in Georgia on December 22. Sherman had completed his "march to the sea."

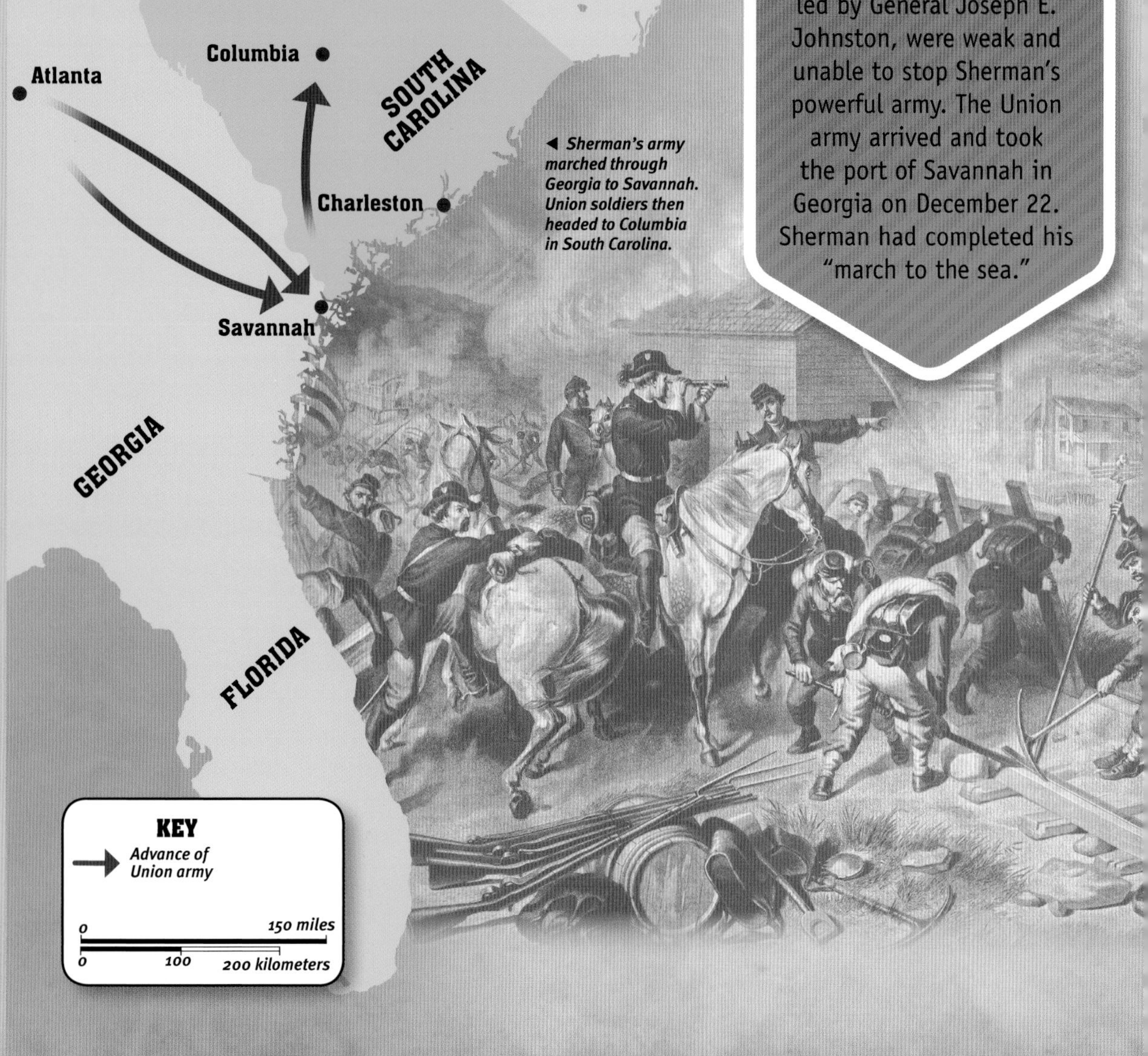

Columbia
Atlanta
SOUTH CAROLINA
Charleston
Savannah
GEORGIA
FLORIDA
KEY
Advance of Union army
0
150 miles
0
100
200 kilometers

◄ *Sherman's army marched through Georgia to Savannah. Union soldiers then headed to Columbia in South Carolina.*

SHERMAN DISAPPEARS

During the march, Sherman also decided to cut off communication with his leaders, including President Lincoln and General Grant. Lincoln said, "I know what hole he went in at, but I can't tell you what hole he'll come out of."

▲ General Sherman and officers stand next to a cannon as they besiege Atlanta in Georgia in 1864.

CHRISTMAS GIFT

On the day he occupied Savannah, Sherman sent a telegram to President Lincoln: "I beg to present to you, as a Christmas gift, the city of Savannah, with 150 guns and plenty of ammunition, and also about 25,000 bales of cotton." Lincoln immediately thanked him, ending his message with "But what next?"

SHERMAN THE DESTROYER

Sherman ordered that civilians should be unharmed in Georgia, but he allowed his troops to steal supplies. They took possessions from the frightened Georgians and burned cotton fields and buildings. Much of Atlanta, Georgia's capital city, was destroyed. The *Macon Telegraph*, a Georgia newspaper, called Sherman "The desolator of our homes, the destroyer of our property, the Attila of the west."

▲ A street corner in Atlanta with a destroyed bank building. Atlanta was pounded by Union forces and fell on September 2, 1864.

WHAT CAME NEXT?

After sweeping through Georgia, Sherman turned his attention to South Carolina. He reached Columbia on February 17, 1865. There, his soldiers set fire to many buildings and homes. He then planned to go to Charleston, but the city had already fallen to Union forces. So, Sherman headed toward North Carolina and arrived at its capital, Raleigh, four days after Lee had surrendered his Army of Northern Virginia. On April 26, Sherman accepted the surrender of General Johnston. The war was finally at an end.

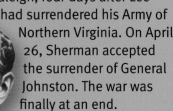

◀ Confederate General Joseph Johnston, who later became friends with his opponent, General Sherman.

▲ Soldiers burned buildings and destroyed railroad tracks and telegraph poles during their march through Georgia.

41

March to the music

Soldiers on both sides marched to rousing band music. They also played instruments and sang around campfires. Tunes ranged from great patriotic pieces such as "Dixie" and "The Battle Hymn of the Republic" to songs about family and sweethearts back home.

▲ Soldiers march and sing "The Battle Hymn of the Republic" in front of a portrait of Julia Ward Howe.

REBEL ANTHEM

Daniel Decatur Emmett from Ohio wrote the spirited song "Dixie" for a New York minstrel show in the 1850s. It became a great hit across the U.S., until it became the unofficial anthem and nickname of the South.

I wish I was in the land of cotton,
Old times there are not forgotten;
Look away! Look away! Look away, Dixie's land!
Then I wish I was in Dixie! Hooray! Hooray!
In Dixie's Land I'll take my stand,
to live and die in Dixie!
Away! Away! Away down South in Dixie!
Away! Away! Away down South in Dixie!

◄ Daniel Decatur Emmett, the composer of the popular American song "Dixie."

BATTLE HYMN

Julia Ward Howe wrote "The Battle Hymn of the Republic" in the fall of 1861 after she heard marching soldiers sing "John Brown's Body" (see page 11). She composed new words to the music for this now-famous song.

Mine eyes have seen the glory
of the coming of the Lord;
He is trampling out the
vintage where the grapes
of wrath are stored;
He hath loosed the fateful
lightning of his terrible
swift sword:
His truth is marching on.
Glory, glory, hallelujah!
Glory, glory, hallelujah!
Glory, glory, hallelujah!
His truth is marching on.

WHY DID LINCOLN LOVE "DIXIE"?

"Dixie," the minstrel song that came to represent the Confederacy, had been a favorite of Abraham Lincoln's before the war. He even used it as his campaign song when running for President in 1860, changing the words to: "At Chicago they selected Lincoln who will be elected, Abraham, Abraham, Abraham, Abraham." When the war ended, he celebrated on the White House balcony in front of around 3,000 people. He requested the band play "Dixie," saying it was "one of the best tunes I ever heard."

▼ *Union volunteers in patriotic dress march along to "Yankee Doodle." In the background is the Potomac River and the skyline of Washington, D.C.*

YANKEE WITHOUT THE DOODLE

"Yankee Doodle" was an old patriotic song loved by both sides. However, it presented problems for those in the South who were fighting the Yankees in the North. When James Chestnut, a South Carolina judge, heard his wife playing "Yankee Doodle" on the piano, he politely asked her to "leave out the Yankee while you play the Doodle."

(30) 1865

The end of the war

Southern troops fought for more than four years in a bid to stop the enemy from taking their capital in Richmond, Virginia. However, on April 2, 1865, the Confederate army was forced to abandon the city. By 11 p.m., President Jefferson Davis and his cabinet had fled by train to Danville, Virginia.

▼ Civilians flee across the James River as Richmond burns behind them.

PANIC AND FIRE

Civilians also had to leave the city. The streets were crowded with frightened people, looters, and drunken soldiers. As the Confederate army left, they blew up ships on the James River and destroyed bridges. Four tobacco warehouses were set on fire. The flames spread through many buildings, and the fire was still burning when Union troops arrived the next morning.

KEY EVENTS

★ **April 2, 1865**
The South's capital, Richmond, Virginia, falls as Union armies approach (see above).

★ **April 9, 1895**
General Lee signs the official surrender. He is given generous terms (see pages 46–47).

★ **April 14, 1865**
President Lincoln is assassinated at the theater in Washington, D.C. (see pages 48–49).

★ **April 15, 1865**
Andrew Johnson succeeds Lincoln and begins the process of Reconstruction (see page 50).

LINCOLN TOURS RICHMOND

When he heard about the fall of Richmond, President Lincoln decided he wanted to visit the city. He arrived by ship on April 4 and strolled around Richmond with his son, Tad (who was 12 years old that day). Freed slaves and Union soldiers cheered Lincoln, although many others in the crowd were silent. When some black people fell to their knees in front of him, Lincoln told them, "You must kneel to God only and thank Him for your freedom." He ended the visit by going to the presidential mansion of Davis and sitting at his empty desk.

▲ *President Lincoln is greeted by freed slaves during his ride through Richmond.*

CAPTURE OF DAVIS

From Danville, Davis and his remaining cabinet members continued on to Greensboro, North Carolina, and Washington, Georgia. Davis hoped to continue west of the Mississippi River and continue the war. He was traveling with a cavalry escort, and they were quickly recognized in the Southern towns they passed. On May 10, a detachment of Union cavalry charged his camp in woods near Irwinville, Georgia, and captured Davis along with his wife and those still protecting him.

DISGUISED IN A DRESS?

Newspapers in the North reported that President Davis tried to avoid capture by wearing women's clothes. In fact, his wife had thrown her shawl over his head because of the chilly weather.

▶ *Mocking cartoons of Jefferson Davis in women's clothing were popular in the North.*

July 1865
Union nurse Clara Barton begins work identifying the dead at Andersonville Prison (see page 53).

November 10, 1865
Andersonville Prison commandant Henry Wirz is hanged for harsh conduct (see page 51).

1875
Civil War photographer Mathew Brady sells his archive to the government for $25,000 (see page 57).

1883
General Lee's son Custis Lee sells Arlington House back to the government for $150,000 (see page 54).

General Lee surrenders

By April 1865, the South's war had become hopeless. On April 2, General Grant's strong army defeated General Lee's weakened force at Petersburg, Virginia, where the Confederates had been under siege for 10 months. Many Confederate soldiers, starving and often shoeless, had deserted the lost cause. After another defeat on April 6 at Sayler's Creek, Virginia, Lee had lost a third of his ragged army. Grant sent a request for surrender and Lee grudgingly agreed. The two generals met on April 9 for the official surrender at the village of Appomattox Court House, Virginia.

▼ The site of the village of Appomattox Court House in Virginia.

WEST VIRGINIA

VIRGINIA

Richmond ●

Appomattox Court House ●   Petersburg ●

KEY

● McLean house location

0   150 miles

0   100   200 kilometers

NORTH CAROLINA

THE McLEAN HOUSE

The surrender of Lee's Army of Northern Virginia was signed at the home of Wilmer McLean. McLean had owned a house at Bull Run, but his family was so shaken by the shelling around them that they moved to the quiet Appomattox Court House to avoid the war—only to have the war end in their parlor! After the surrender, Union soldiers bought mementos from McLean, including the table on which the surrender was signed. He refused to sell the two chairs used, so cavalry officers stole them.

At the end of the war, both of Lee's sons were missing in action, but both survived.

THE WAR ENDS

▲ Generals Lee and Grant meet to settle terms of surrender. Grant would later recall, "Our conversation grew so pleasant that I almost forgot the object of our meeting."

When Lee and Grant met, there was no feeling of triumph or humiliation. Both men had served in the U.S. Army and they had fought together in the Mexican War. They talked about old times and Grant would later recall feeling depressed about the downfall of his enemy. Lee was dressed in a new uniform while Grant looked scruffy and his boots were splattered with mud. After signing the document, they shook hands. As they left, they took off their hats to each other as a final salute.

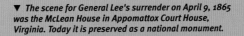

▼ The scene for General Lee's surrender on April 9, 1865 was the McLean House in Appomattox Court House, Virginia. Today it is preserved as a national monument.

GENEROUS TERMS

Following Lincoln's orders, Grant offered Lee generous terms. He allowed all Lee's men to return safely to their homes if they agreed to stop fighting. He also gave them rations and stopped the Union troops from firing victory salutes, saying the Confederates were "our countrymen again" and "we did not want to exult over their downfall."

▲ Union troops standing outside Appomattox Court House after the Confederate surrender.

The death of Lincoln

On April 14, 1865, President Lincoln went to see a play in Washington, D.C. As Lincoln watched the show, an actor named John Wilkes Booth sneaked into the president's private box and shot him in the back of the head. Booth then jumped onto the stage in front of the shocked audience and escaped.

▼ Booth shoots President Lincoln at Ford's Theatre, Washington, D.C. Booth had supported the Confederacy.

Lincoln had strange dreams about being murdered just days before he was shot.

LUCKY ESCAPE

General Grant and his wife had been invited to sit with the Lincolns to watch the play, but they were unable to attend. Their places were taken by Major Henry Rathbone and his fiancée. When Booth shot the president, Rathbone wrestled with him and Booth stabbed him in the arm.

◀ The dagger used by Booth to stab Major Henry Rathbone after shooting President Abraham Lincoln.

WHAT
HAPPENED NEXT?

A surgeon in the audience immediately went to Lincoln and saw that the wound was fatal. Soldiers carried Lincoln to a nearby **boarding house** and placed him on a bed. The President remained unconscious and died the next morning at 7:22 a.m.

▼ *Abraham Lincoln lies dying in bed, surrounded by cabinet members, generals, and his weeping wife, Mary.*

FINDING THE ASSASSIN

John Wilkes Booth was on the run for 12 days until Union soldiers cornered him in a tobacco barn in Virginia. He refused to surrender. The soldiers, who had orders to take him alive, set the barn on fire. But when Booth ran out, an excited sergeant shot him. As he was dying, Booth whispered, "Tell my mother I died for my country." Four others were convicted of helping him, including one woman, and were later hanged.

▲ *The murderer John Wilkes Booth is seized by Union soldiers.*

THE FUNERAL TRAIN

A special funeral train took Lincoln's body from Washington, D.C. to his home in Springfield, Illinois, for burial. The train passed slowly through seven states, covering 1,662 miles in 14 days. Millions of mourners along the route were able to honor the fallen president. Lincoln's body also lay in state in Philadelphia, New York, and Cleveland.

MORE PLOTS

Booth and two other men had planned more **assassinations** to happen at the same time. One man was to shoot Vice President Andrew Johnson, but he became nervous and backed out. Another was to kill Secretary of State William Seward. The attacker did stab and wound Seward and his two sons, but he then ran outside yelling, "I'm mad! I'm mad!"

▲ *Secretary of State William Seward was stabbed but survived the assassination attempt.*

President Johnson

Andrew Johnson became the nation's leader when Lincoln was assassinated. He was a former owner of slaves and governor of Tennessee. As President, he tried to follow Lincoln's program of **Reconstruction**, designed to rebuild the ruined South. Radical Republicans, however, wanted to punish the South. In 1864, they took Johnson to court, a process known as impeachment.

◄ *President Andrew Johnson was born in poverty in South Carolina in 1808.*

ACCOMPLISHMENTS

During President Johnson's administration two **Constitutional** Amendments became law. The 13th Amendment abolished slavery (see page 61) and the 14th Amendment turned former slaves and others born in the United States into citizens (see page 64).

THE IMPEACHMENT

Radical Republicans thought that Johnson's type of Reconstruction was too kind. They wanted the former Confederate states punished, but Johnson kept rejecting their demands. They opened an impeachment trial in 1868, using the excuse that Johnson had removed the Secretary of War without notifying the Senate. Johnson escaped conviction but he failed to get a nomination for a second term as President the following year.

▲ *The impeachment trial of Andrew Johnson was held at the U.S. Senate and lasted two months.*

Andersonville Prison

The end of the war also saw public anger in the North over the treatment of Union soldiers in prisons. The Confederacy's largest prison was Camp Sumter in Georgia, also called Andersonville Prison. Conditions were so bad that almost 13,000 died there, often from disease, starvation, and lack of shelter.

THE DEAD LINE

The prison had a long rail on posts set 19 feet inside the stockade wall. It was known as the "dead line" because any prisoner passing it was shot, even if they were only reaching for water or pieces of food.

▼ *The stockade wall at Andersonville Prison, Georgia. The dead line was erected inside in order to keep prisoners away from the stockade.*

UNION PRISONS

Captured Confederates also suffered and died in some unhealthy Union prisons. Horrible conditions in Elmira Prison in New York state, nicknamed "Hellmira," resulted in 2,963 deaths from freezing weather and malnutrition. Camp Douglas in Illinois, called the "Andersonville of the North," recorded 4,200 deaths.

THE COMMANDANT

Henry Wirz was made the commandant of Andersonville Prison on March 27, 1864. At the war's end, he was convicted for his harsh conduct and hanged, becoming the only Confederate officer to be executed.

◄ *Henry Wirz was born in Switzerland and came to the U.S. in 1861.*

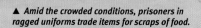
▲ *Amid the crowded conditions, prisoners in ragged uniforms trade items for scraps of food.*

Andersonville was built to hold 10,000 men but 45,000 were imprisoned there.

Women and the war

In the 19th century, the usual role of women during wartime was to provide support from home, sending letters and gifts to soldiers, or raising a family alone. However, many women on both sides took a more active part in the Civil War. These included nurses, spies, government clerks, abolitionists, and writers. Some even dressed as men to fight as soldiers.

HARRIET BEECHER STOWE

Before the war, Stowe and her husband, the Reverend Calvin Stowe, made their home a safe house for runaway slaves escaping along the Underground Railroad (see page 22). She wrote a novel called *Uncle Tom's Cabin* about the harsh lives of slaves on a plantation. First published in the 1850s, the book described the cruelty of slavery in the South.

◀ *Author Harriet Beecher Stowe. Her book,* Uncle Tom's Cabin, *was a bestselling novel in the 19th century.*

Stowe's Uncle Tom's Cabin sold over 1 million copies in the first year of publication.

ROSE O'NEAL GREENHOW

Greenhow was a society hostess in Washington, D.C., who became a spy for the Confederacy. She tipped off General Beauregard about Union activity before the Battle of Bull Run (see page 17). Placed under house arrest, she continued to spy with her daughter. Both were sent to prison in 1862, and then banished to Richmond, Virginia. President Davis told her, "But for you, there would have been no Battle of Bull Run."

▲ *Rose Greenhow wrote her messages in secret code, as shown in this letter.*

FEMALE SOLDIER

Frances Clalin Clayton joined the Union army by disguising herself as a man and changing her name to Jack Williams. She fought at several battles, including Williamsburg and the Second Battle of Bull Run (see page 17). Once, she disguised herself as a saleswoman so she could spy behind Confederate lines. Clayton fell sick with malaria in 1863 and escaped back to Union forces to avoid detection by doctors. She then became a nurse in Washington, D.C. until the end of the war.

▶ Frances Clalin Clayton, wearing women's clothing in 1865. She told reporters that she was never discovered as a woman when she fought in the Civil War.

▲ Frances Clalin Clayton, disguised as a man and enlisted in a Missouri regiment.

CLARA BARTON

When the war broke out, Clara Barton left her work as a clerk to nurse Union soldiers. She became known as the "Angel of the Battlefield." Lincoln had her gather information on missing and dead soldiers so their relatives could be contacted. After the war, she spent four years identifying the dead at Andersonville Prison. In 1877, Barton founded the American Red Cross.

Arlington National Cemetery

Arlington House was the name of Robert E. Lee's home just across the Potomac River from Washington, D.C. It was seized by the U.S. government after the war began and became a headquarters for the Union army. In June 1864, Union General Montgomery Meigs chose Arlington as the site for a new military cemetery. It was thought a good location and would also punish Lee for deserting to the Confederacy.

▲ Robert E. Lee's former home, Arlington House. Union soldiers are on the front steps.

AFTER THE WAR

Lee's oldest son, Custis Lee, who had been a Confederate general, sued the U.S. Government for having confiscated the house. The Supreme Court ruled in his favor in 1882. The house was returned to the family, but in 1883 he sold it back to the government for $150,000.

▼ Tombstones at Arlington. The first graves were placed close to the front door of the house.

ARLINGTON TODAY

More than 400,000 people who have served the nation in war, including nearly 5,000 unknown soldiers, are buried on the cemetery's 624 acres. President John F. Kennedy is also buried here and Arlington's other special features include the Tomb of the Unknown Soldier and the Memorial Amphitheater. More than 4 million people visit the cemetery each year.

Read all about it

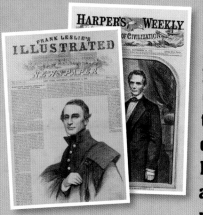

▲ *Popular newspapers from the era of the Civil War. By 1860, most U.S. cities published newspapers.*

The inventions of the telegraph and rotary press resulted in newspapers with large circulations. They brought news of the war to eager readers. *Harper's Weekly* carried detailed drawings of battle scenes. Military leaders urged journalists to cover victories and other good news, but they disliked negative reporting.

HORACE GREELEY

Greeley launched the *New York Tribune* and influenced the public and politicians, though he often changed his own opinions. He said the Union should let the South secede, then pushed for attacks on Richmond. When the war ended, Greeley caused outrage when he signed the bail bond for President Davis, releasing him from jail.

▶ *Newspaper editor Horace Greeley also ran for President in 1872.*

▶ *William Howard Russell was considered one of the first modern war reporters.*

WILLIAM HOWARD RUSSELL

Russell was a famous British war journalist who covered the Civil War. He visited Lincoln, who said of his newspaper, *The Times*, "I don't know anything which has much more power—except the Mississippi." Russell traveled through the South and his favorable reports of the Confederates angered the North. His reports of the Union troops' desperate flight at Bull Run (see page 17) led to him being banned from traveling with the Union army.

William Howard Russell also reported on the Crimean War in the 1850s.

Photography

The Civil War was the first conflict that was photographed. The world's first combat photo was taken by Southern photographer George Cook, who took a picture of ironclads firing at Fort Moultrie, South Carolina, in September 1863. However, the war's best-known photographer was Mathew Brady. He took more than 3,500 photos in dangerous conditions, traveling with the Union armies. Exhibitions of Brady's battlefield photos shocked the Northern public.

▲ *An early war photo: Major Robert Anderson, by Mathew Brady.*

THE DEVELOPING PROCESS

Brady developed his photos using a system of chemicals and glass plates, which he carried with him as he followed the armies. He converted his buggy into a covered "dark wagon" to develop the photographs. This strange vehicle was nicknamed "the Whatisit" by soldiers.

▲ *A wartime photograph of a young private named Henry Wright.*

PORTRAITS

Before the war, Brady had portrait studios in New York and Washington, D.C. Almost all of the Union's leaders stopped by to have their portraits taken, including President Lincoln. Ordinary soldiers also posed for inexpensive card-sized photos known as *cartes de visite* (visiting cards), which they gave to their families and sweethearts. After the war, Brady even photographed Robert E. Lee, whom he had known before the fighting began.

SITTING FOR A PORTRAIT

Early photographs required the subject to sit still for the camera's long exposure time. Portrait studios had chairs equipped with a neck clamp to hold a sitter's head still. This was uncomfortable and photographers needed charm to put customers at ease. Lincoln was said to look weary waiting for equipment to be set up, and General Sherman's impatience is clear in this photo.

◄ *General Sherman manages to sit still for his photograph.*

"THE DEAD OF ANTIETAM"

Brady's exhibitions brought Northerners face-to-face with the horror of war. The most-viewed display was in October 1862 at Brady's New York studio. Called "The Dead of Antietam," it showed images of the battle that had taken place on September 17. These were the first photographs of dead soldiers seen by the public. They turned some people against the war.

◄ *Photographers with their equipment wagon In 1864. The man sitting on the left is David Woodbury, who worked for Mathew Brady.*

▶ *"The father of photojournalism," Mathew Brady, in 1875.*

WHAT HAPPENED TO BRADY?

After the South surrendered, people wanted to forget the tragedy of the war. Brady's photographs became less popular, and he went bankrupt in 1873. He sold his collection in 1875 for $25,000 to the U.S. Government, which preserved it in the Library of Congress.

The losses

More Americans died in the Civil War than in any other conflict, including World War II. Deaths on the battlefield were high, although twice as many men died from disease. Unhealthy, crowded conditions in the camps were often to blame. Soldiers fought in freezing weather and torrential rain. They ate rotting food, and unsanitary toilet pits and garbage led to epidemics.

DEADLY DISEASES

▼ *The Armory Square Hospital in Washington, D.C. in 1865. This "pavilion" hospital had high standards, and was visited by President Lincoln several times.*

Among the worst diseases that killed soldiers were dysentery, pneumonia, typhoid fever, tuberculosis, diphtheria, malaria, yellow fever, and scurvy. Common epidemics included measles, smallpox, chicken pox, mumps, whooping cough, and influenza.

In the South, 18 percent of all white men aged between 13 and 43 died in the war.

KEY EVENTS

★ **January 31, 1865**
The 13th Amendment is approved and the postwar work of rebuilding begins (see pages 60–61).

★ **May 9, 1865**
By the time the end of the war is announced, battlefield losses are very high (see above).

★ **December 24, 1865**
The white supremacist Ku Klux Klan is founded in the South by six Confederate veterans (see pages 62–63).

★ **April 9, 1866**
The Civil Rights Act is passed protecting African Americans but the country remains divided (see pages 64–65).

HOW MANY DIED?

The general estimate is that 618,222 soldiers died in the Civil War. Of these, 360,222 were in the Union army and 258,000 in the Confederate one. New research in 2011 updated the total to 750,000, although it is always difficult to give exact figures for battle casualties. The larger Union total was partially due to better reporting and to General Grant's tactic of wearing down the enemy. He had a bigger army than the South, so dead soldiers could be replaced.

Estimated casualties (killed and wounded) for some of the worst Civil War battles:

	Union	Confederate
Shiloh	13,047	10,699
Antietam	12,410	13,724
Fredericksburg	13,000	5,300
Chancellorsville	17,278	12,821
Gettysburg	23,049	28,063
Chickamauga	16,179	18,454

▶ Soldiers' Cemetery, Alexandria, Virginia. Founded in 1862, it may have been one of the first Civil War cemeteries.

BATTLEFIELD BURIALS

The numbers killed during battles were too high for proper burials. The work usually fell to the victorious army, who might leave bodies of the enemy unburied. Items were removed from the dead. Poorly supplied Confederates took guns, shoes, and other necessities. Armies on the move often dug trenches for mass burials. On some occasions, the two sides would agree to a truce during a battle in order to remove the bodies of those killed during the day.

THE DEAD AT SHILOH

"In places dead men lay so closely that a person could walk over two acres of ground and not step off the bodies."

John Bell, 2nd Iowa Volunteers, 1862

November 3, 1868
General Ulysses S. Grant is elected the 18th President of the United States (see page 66).

May 18, 1896
The Supreme Court upholds segregation laws, using the words "separate but equal" (see pages 70–71).

August 28, 1963
Martin Luther King addresses the largest ever civil rights march in Washington (see page 72).

November 4, 2007
Barack Obama is elected the 44th President of the United States (see page 75).

Aftermath and Reconstruction

Lincoln had not wanted harsh punishment for the defeated South. President Johnson was even more lenient with the former Confederates. Radical Republicans, however, managed to override Johnson and set up a military occupation in the South that lasted 12 years, until 1877.

▲ *"Carpetbaggers" were named after the large carpet bags they carried with all their possessions.*

CARPETBAGGERS AND SCALAWAGS

Northerners, known as "carpetbaggers," flooded into the South during Reconstruction. Many came to help former slaves by setting up schools or helping them find work. Some came to take advantage of cheap land. Southerners who supported the Reconstruction or the Republican Party were criticized by people in the South and called "scalawags."

REJOINING THE UNION

Former Confederate states were not automatically returned to the Union. A state could only return to the Union after 10 percent of its population had taken an oath of loyalty to the United States. The tough Reconstruction plan also denied office to former Confederate leaders and assured the vote for former slaves. Louisiana became the last state to rejoin the United States in 1877.

▲ *During the conflict, prisoners of war were often released after taking an oath of allegiance to the Union.*

Slavery abolished

The United States had fought the war to preserve the Union and to abolish slavery. The defeat of the Confederacy had preserved the Union, but the Emancipation Proclamation had failed to abolish slavery everywhere in the United States. This would be achieved by the 13th Amendment to the Constitution, which was finally approved by Congress on January 31, 1865.

▶ African-American men wait in line to vote. The 15th Amendment of 1870 gave them this right.

WHAT DID IT SAY?

The short amendment had two paragraphs freeing slaves and enforcing the law:

1. *Neither slavery nor involuntary servitude, except as a punishment of crime whereof the party should have been duly convicted, shall exist within the United States, or any place subject to their jurisdiction.*

2. *Congress shall have power to enforce this article by appropriate legislation.*

A LATE RATIFICATION

The amendment needed three-quarters of the 36 states to give consent to it. That goal was reached when Georgia **ratified** it on December 6, 1865. Slavery was now legally abolished. Mississippi held out, wanting to be reimbursed for the value of the freed slaves. It did ratify the amendment in 1995, but an administration error meant that this wasn't made official until February 27, 2013.

▲ An illustration of a freed slave dressed in ragged clothing rejoicing.

The Proclamation stopped anti-slavery European powers helping the Confederates.

Black Codes

▲ The Ku Klux Klan at work in 1868. Dressed in normal clothes, they are shown murdering the Radical Republican George W. Ashburn for his support of African Americans.

In 1864 and 1865, the Southern states passed laws that restricted the newly freed slaves. These were known as the "Black Codes." They were overturned by Radical Republicans, but whites in the South continued to deny equal political and social rights to African Americans. This would later develop into formal racial **segregation** in the South.

RESTRICTIONS

The Black Codes restricted the freedom of former slaves in a number of ways. They included restrictions on the right to vote, hold certain property, carry firearms, have equal schooling, sit on juries, and testify in court against whites. They also restricted free movement in certain public spaces, required ex-slaves to hold a steady job, and forced them to sign strict labor contracts.

▲ The KKK emblem shows a cross with a drop of red blood in the center.

THE KLAN BEGINS

As soon as the war ended, Southerners began to look for ways to regain control over their new circumstances. Some people set up secret societies to maintain white supremacy. The most infamous, the Ku Klux Klan (KKK), was founded on December 24, 1865, by six Confederate veterans. They called themselves the Invisible Empire and the former Confederate general Nathan Bedford Forrest became the first leader, or Grand Wizard.

WHAT DID THE KLAN DO?

The Ku Klux Klan wanted to intimidate newly freed slaves. At first, the members used practical jokes to cause fear. The KKK would ride to their houses at night wearing their white robes and pointed hoods. One trick was for a Klansman to ask for water and seem to drink buckets of it using a hose under his robe. These jokes, however, soon grew into violence such as arson, beatings, and **lynchings**.

▲ An African-American family at home. They are unaware that a hooded Ku Klux Klan member is standing at the door with a rifle.

NATHAN BEDFORD FORREST

Forrest was a Confederate general and one of the most revengeful against African Americans. Reports said that he ordered his men to shoot black Union soldiers as they attempted to surrender at the Battle of Fort Pillow. Later, however, he changed his mind and tried to disband the KKK, and in 1875 he supported the education of former slaves.

▶ General Forrest, who was said to have overseen a massacre of black soldiers.

▲ A meeting of the Ku Klux Klan in 1920. By 1924, the KKK had between 1.5 to 4 million members in the U.S.

Equal rights

As they took control of Congress, the Radical Republicans moved quickly to secure equal rights for African Americans. The 1866 Civil Rights Act protected their **civil rights**. They also passed the 14th and 15th Amendments that, with the 13th, were known as the three Reconstruction Amendments.

THE AMENDMENTS

Passed in June 1866 and ratified in July 1868, the 14th Amendment forbade any state to deprive any person of "life, liberty, or property" or to deny any person "equal protection of the laws." The short 15th Amendment, passed in February 1869 and ratified in February 1870, said that voting rights could "not be denied or abridged by the United States or by any State on account of race, color, or previous condition of servitude."

◀ *A representative of the Freedmen's Bureau (see page 65) stands between angry groups of white men and freed slaves.*

THADDEUS STEVENS

Thaddeus Stevens was the founder and leader of the Radical Republicans in the U.S. House of Representatives. During the war, he had urged Lincoln to "free every slave, slay every traitor, burn every Rebel mansion." He helped to create the severe Reconstruction plan, calling the South a "conquered province."

▶ *Radical Republican Thaddeus Stevens believed the South should be heavily punished for the war.*

Abraham Lincoln once described the United States as "half slave and half free."

A nation still divided

The South was poorer in resources and manpower than the North. Industries and businesses in Northern cities were boosted by the wartime economy, while many of the major Southern towns were in ruins. Southern agriculture had been devastated by the loss of slaves and the Union army's tactic of burning crops.

▲ The ruins of a railroad depot in Charleston, South Carolina.

▶ A thriving Northern factory in Portland, Maine. A railroad passenger train passes by.

THE FREEDMEN'S BUREAU

Supported by President Lincoln, this bureau was established in 1865 for one year by Congress to help "destitute and suffering refugees and freedmen and their wives and children." It provided freed slaves with land, food, clothing, and fuel. It also built schools and hospitals, and provided relief for poor whites. The bureau lasted until 1872.

DEFEAT AND DIVISION

Southerners either accepted the defeat or remained bitter. Robert E. Lee was eager to reestablish peace and harmony in the South. Many refused, keeping their dislike for "damn Yankees," and many Northerners never forgave their countrymen for causing the war.

◀ African Americans in need of poor relief gather outside the Freedmen's Bureau in Richmond, Virginia.

Eleven cities in the South were destroyed or severely damaged in the Civil War.

44

65

What became of them?

After the war, most soldiers returned to their former lives. Others remained in the military, and some former Confederate troops even joined Union forces in the Indian Wars against Native Americans. Politicians who had made their name during the war were rewarded by voters and continued to serve the country.

GENERAL GRANT

General Ulysses S. Grant (1822–1885) served as Secretary of War for five months until 1868 when he was elected the nation's 18th President. He was reelected in 1872. In 1881, Grant became a partner in his son's business in New York but it collapsed, leaving him penniless. Suffering from cancer, he then wrote his memoirs and died days after finishing the final page.

▲ *General Grant on the porch of his home at Mount McGregor, New York, where he spent his last days.*

▲ *Robert Edward Lee in May, 1869.*

GENERAL LEE

General Robert E. Lee (1807–1870) retired briefly to Richmond, Virginia. In the fall of 1865, he became President of Washington College (now Washington and Lee College) in Lexington, Virginia. He refused offers to write his memoirs and spent his last years appealing to Southerners to show good will and accept their united country. His former soldiers, as well as previous enemies, were frequent visitors to his office.

PRESIDENT DAVIS

After Jefferson Davis (1808–1889) was captured, he was imprisoned in Fort Monroe in Hampton, Virginia. Here, he was shackled in solitary confinement. Released in 1867, he traveled to Canada and England. He became President of an insurance company in Memphis, Tennessee. He retired in 1877 near Biloxi, Mississippi, where he wrote a history of the Confederate government and made speeches to justify the South's cause.

◄ *Jefferson Davis at his retirement home near Biloxi, Mississippi, in 1885.*

GENERAL SHERMAN

General William Tecumseh Sherman (1820–1891) remained in the army after the war. He went to St. Louis to help subdue the Native Americans and to build a railroad crossing the U.S. In 1869, President Grant promoted him to commander-in-chief of the army. He retired to New York City in 1884 and published two volumes of memoirs.

◄ *William Tecumseh Sherman in 1888.*

◄ *General George Armstrong Custer's Last Stand at the Battle of Little Bighorn, 1876*

GENERAL CUSTER

General George Armstrong Custer (1839–1876) was a Union cavalry commander in the Civil War. He later led a major defeat of the Cheyenne Indian tribe in Oklahoma. In 1876, he fought the Cheyenne and Lakota Sioux. Custer and his men were massacred in what is known as "Custer's Last Stand."

HARRIET TUBMAN

When the war ended, Tubman (1821–1913) settled in Auburn, New York, and traveled to promote women's rights. She donated part of her land in 1903 to build a home for elderly "colored people." She saw the Harriet Tubman Home for the Aged open in 1908.

▶ *Harriet Tubman at her home in Auburn, New York, in 1911.*

46

Native Americans

Around 20,000 Native Americans fought on both sides during the war. Many favored the Confederacy against the U.S. Army, whose government was taking their lands. Key leaders included Stand Watie for the Cherokees fighting for the Confederacy, and Ely Parker, a Seneca friend and secretary of General Grant. Military service by Native Americans brought them very little benefit.

▲ Two Oglala chiefs, American Horse (left) and Red Cloud, shaking hands in front of a tipi, on the Pine Ridge Reservation in 1891.

CHEROKEES

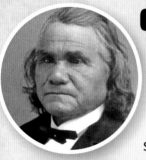

▲ Stand Watie was the only Native American general in the Confederate army.

The Cherokees planned to remain neutral when the war began, but gave their support to the Confederacy when it promised them special rights for fighting on their side. Some Cherokees owned their own slaves. In 1862, part of the Cherokee Nation switched their support to Union forces who by then occupied most of the Indian Territory. Those led by Stand Watie, however, remained loyal to the South.

STAND WATIE

Born in Oothcaloga (now north Georgia), Watie became a farmer and a journalist. In 1861, he was made a colonel commanding a cavalry unit mostly made up of Cherokee Indians. Although defeated at the Battle of Pea Ridge in Arkansas in March 1862, Cherokee bravery was noted—they charged an artillery battery, and Union troops reported that 30 of their men had been scalped. During the war, Watie led his men in 18 battles and skirmishes. He was promoted to brigadier general in May 1864, the highest ranking Native American in the war.

▶ Wounded Native American soldiers, probably from Company K of the 1st Michigan Sharpshooters, rest after the Battle of Fredericksburg.

ELY S. PARKER

Born Ha-sa-no-an-da on a Seneca **reservation** at Indian Falls, New York, Parker took his westernized name when he was still at school. He earned a degree and met General Grant when he was working as a civil engineer. He was told he couldn't sign up for the war, but Grant helped him join as an engineer. In 1864, Grant made him his military secretary and promoted him to the rank of lieutenant colonel. Parker was with Grant at the surrender of Appomattox (see pages 46–47) and helped draft the official paperwork. When informed he was a Seneca, Lee said, "I am glad to see one real American here," to which Parker replied, "We are all Americans."

▲ Lieutenant Colonel Ely S. Parker (right) sits with General John A. Rawlins, General Grant's chief of staff, outside Grant's headquarters.

SHARPSHOOTERS

The Union's most renowned Native-American unit was Company K of the 1st Michigan Sharpshooters. It was made up of marksmen from the Delaware, Ottawa, Ojibwa, Potawami, and Huron Oneida. In 1864, under General Grant, they captured some 600 enemy troops near Petersburg in Virginia.

Jim Crow laws

Most recreational places, such as parks, fairs, pools, and zoos, were off limits to blacks.

After the 1866 Civil Rights Act was passed to protect African Americans' rights, Southerners introduced segregation. This came in the form of the Jim Crow laws (named after a black character in minstrel shows). It separated African Americans from whites except when working as employees. Even the U.S. Supreme Court approved. In an 1896 ruling, it stated that "separate but equal" was legal. The "equal" promise was almost never kept.

▶ A man drinks at a "colored" water cooler in a streetcar terminal in 1939.

WHAT WAS SEPARATED?

Signs for "White" and "Colored" areas existed in bus and train stations, movie theaters (blacks in the balcony), and restrooms. When allowed on public transportation, blacks were restricted to designated sections such as the back of the bus. Facilities such as water fountains were also marked by race. Some buildings even had "White" and "Colored" elevators. Restaurants, hotels, and schools were designated for one race or the other. Sports teams were segregated.

AFRICAN-AMERICAN JOBS

Segregation kept African Americans from holding any important jobs. Some positions were only given to blacks. Among the most respected of these jobs were railroad conductors and red caps (baggage porters) for men, while the best jobs for women were in homes as a maid or nanny (normally called "mammy") for white children.

▲ African-American trolley car conductors in Philadelphia, Pennsylvania in 1940.

Toward the end of the 1800s, the term "New South" was used to mean a new society and economy that would boost the region. However, it also implied the new segregation. Some African Americans saw opportunities to use the system to make their own success. Booker T. Washington, an educator from Virginia, advised blacks to work with the segregationists, saying that "we can be as separate as the five fingers, yet one as the hand in all things essential to mutual progress." He achieved this by building Alabama's famous black college, Tuskegee Institute. Even so, segregation remained a key issue well into the last half of the 20th century.

► Booker T. Washington in 1910.

SEGREGATION OF BLACK AND WHITE

Segregation did not officially exist in the Union states, but an informal understanding kept the races mostly apart. African Americans were not normally welcomed to white social events and lived in **ghettos** (city slum areas) where they went to all-black schools. They were not part of national radio and television programs. The U.S. military had segregated troops by race during the Civil War, and it continued doing this in World War II. President Harry Truman ordered their integration in 1947, but this was not totally achieved until 1954.

► Major James A. Ellison salutes Tuskegee Airmen, African-American military pilots and crew who fought in World War II.

The civil rights movement

During his campaign of civil disobedience, Martin Luther King was jailed 29 times.

72

There had been a movement for equal rights in one form or another since the Civil War. However, almost a century after the Civil War, many African Americans were still not entitled to vote, and racist crimes often went unpunished. The big boost for equality came from the 1954 Supreme Court ruling that the "separate but equal" doctrine could not exist in education. This would end segregation in all areas, and whites resisted it violently.

◀ *Martin Luther King promoted nonviolent civil disobedience based on his Christian beliefs.*

MARTIN LUTHER KING

Leading the civil rights movement was the brave and inspirational **minister** Martin Luther King, Jr. When Rosa Parks, an African-American woman, was arrested for refusing to give up her seat to a white man on a bus in Montgomery, Alabama, King spoke up for her. He urged passive (nonviolent) resistance. He led a boycott of the buses in 1955, which ended segregation on the buses. On August 28, 1963, he led more than 200,000 people for the March on Washington, the largest ever U.S. demonstration for civil rights. This ended at the Lincoln Memorial, where King gave his famous "I have a dream" speech. On April 4, 1968, he was assassinated in Memphis, Tennessee, by a white gunman.

▶ *Rosa Parks in November 1956, a year after her arrest.*

▲ *The 2857 bus on which Rosa Parks was riding prior to her arrest, now preserved in the Henry Ford Museum in Michigan.*

THE SELMA MARCH

Many civil rights activists traveled to the South to demonstrate and were joined by blacks and sympathetic whites. In Alabama in March 1965, Martin Luther King organized three marches from Selma to Montgomery to support the registration of black voters. One marcher was murdered and many beaten on the first two marches. Thousands of U.S. soldiers and Alabama National Guardsmen protected the third march, which ended in Montgomery on March 25 with a gathering of about 25,000 people.

▼ *Demonstrators carrying American flags march from Selma to Montgomery, Alabama, in 1965.*

▲ *Activists stage a sit-in at the U.S. Capitol Building in March 1965.*

OTHER TACTICS

In 1961, civil rights activists known as "Freedom Riders" defied segregation by riding buses through the South. Another goal was to end segregation in eating places. At these "sit-ins," activists would sit down and order food that was then refused. The first was on February 1, 1960, at a Woolworths lunch counter in Greensboro, North Carolina. Under pressure, Woolworths integrated in July. The sit-ins spread quickly around the South. African Americans also began to register at all-white universities. In 1962, around 30,000 troops were brought in to protect the arrival of the first black student at the University of Mississippi.

Flags

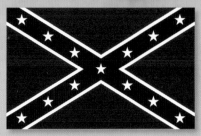

▲ *The Confederate battle flag was designed by General Beauregard.*

The flag associated with the Confederacy is the battle flag. It has a red background and a diagonal blue cross with 13 stars. The Confederacy had 11 states but added stars for Kentucky and Missouri in the hope that they would join. The first national flag of the Confederacy was called the "Stars and Bars."

▲ *The first "Stars and Bars" flag of the Confederacy. It was similar to the U.S. flag but had only three stripes and a circle of seven stars.*

▲ *The Stainless banner (top) and the Blood-stained banner (bottom).*

WHITE FLAGS

The flags of the Union and the Confederacy were similar, which caused confusion at the First Battle of Bull Run. So a second version was designed called the "Stainless Banner." As it was mainly white, it looked like a flag of surrender. So it was replaced by the "Blood-stained Banner" which added a red vertical bar on the side.

THE AMERICAN FLAG

The Union flag was the national flag of the U.S., also known as the Stars and Stripes. Today, the 50 stars represent the 50 states of the United States of America and the 13 stripes represent the 13 British colonies that declared independence from Great Britain in 1776.

▶ *The national flag of America as it appears today.*

The battle flag is also known as the Dixie flag, rebel flag, and Southern Cross.

A black president

The election of Barack Obama as the nation's 44th President in 2008 and his reelection in 2012 highlighted the progress of African Americans in the United States. Millions around the world viewed his election as a historic achievement.

WHAT HE SAID WHEN ELECTED

"If there is anyone out there who still doubts that America is a place where all things are possible; who still wonders if the dream of our founders is alive in our time; who still questions the power of our democracy, tonight is your answer."

Chicago, November 4, 2008

POLITICAL SUCCESS

Born in Honolulu, Hawaii, Obama was elected as U.S. Senator in 2004. As President, he continued to promote racial harmony along with his First Lady, Michelle, who also campaigned for women's rights across the world.

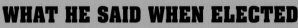

▲ Muriel Bowser, as eighth Mayor of the District of Columbia, has achieved political success.

▲ Mae Carol Jemison became the first African-American woman to travel in space in 1992.

ROLE MODELS

African Americans across the United States have achieved success in every field, from technology, science, and business to the arts and sports. In government, African Americans have achieved major influence and in recent years, those elected in the South's former Confederate states include Supreme Court justices, governors, mayors, and many more.

President Obama was awarded the Nobel Peace Prize in 2009.

WHO'S WHO?
The Civil War

The Civil War featured some of the most remarkable figures in the history of the United States. Both sides had brilliant commanders and both sides fought with bravery. The Confederate General Lee and Union General Grant had great respect for one other and appreciated each other's abilities. Here are some of the most notable figures.

**Jefferson Davis
(1808–1889)**

▨ Confederate President who selected Lee to lead the South's armies and gave him much support.

**Robert E. Lee
(1807–1870)**

▨ As General of the Army of Northern Virginia, Lee's superior tactics won many important victories.

**P. G. T. Beauregard
(1818–1893)**

▨ Beauregard was in command of the guns that started the war by firing on Fort Sumter.

**Thomas "Stonewall" Jackson
(1824–1863)**

▨ Known as the South's finest strategist, Jackson's Virginia victories kept Richmond safe.

**Joseph Johnston
(1807–1891)**

▨ Commander at the victory of Bull Run. He delayed Sherman's advance through Georgia and North Carolina.

**J. E. B. "Jeb" Stuart
(1833–1864)**

▨ General whose cavalry became renowned for raids that encircled Union armies.

**Abraham Lincoln
(1809–1865)**

President of the United States from 1861–1865. His Emancipation Proclamation freed the slaves.

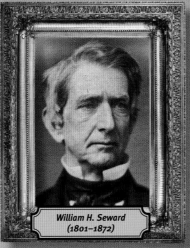

**William H. Seward
(1801–1872)**

William Henry Seward was President Lincoln's Secretary of State from 1861–1869.

**Ulysses S. Grant
(1822–1885)**

Grant was an outstanding military leader who became General-in-Chief and accepted Lee's surrender.

**David Farragut
(1801–1870)**

Naval officer who became an admiral after capturing New Orleans and winning the Battle of Mobile Bay.

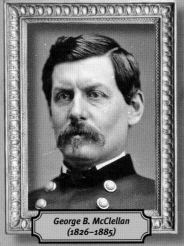

**George B. McClellan
(1826–1885)**

Lincoln's first General-in-Chief who failed to attack several times. Lincoln replaced him.

**Philip Sheridan
(1831–1888)**

Union commander who won at Chattanooga. He carried out a ruthless "scorched earth" campaign.

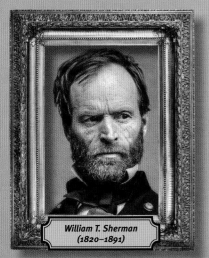

**William T. Sherman
(1820–1891)**

Sherman was a friend of Grant and captured Atlanta. He also won fame for his march to the sea.

**Horace Greeley
(1811–1872)**

Owner of the *New York Tribune* who had great influence on public opinion during the war.

**Harriet Tubman
(c. 1822–1913)**

An escaped slave who became active in the Underground Railroad, helping many others to escape.

GLOSSARY

ABOLITIONIST
Someone who wants to put an end to something, such as slavery.

AMPUTATION
The procedure of cutting off a limb.

ANESTHETIC
A substance that causes the loss of feeling in all or parts of the body.

ARMORY
A place where weapons, especially guns, are manufactured or stored.

ARTILLERY
Large heavy weapons, such as cannons, built to fire solid or explosive shells.

ASSASSINATION
The murder of an important person, usually for political reasons.

BOARDING HOUSE
A house where lodgers rent rooms, often for long periods.

CABINET
The key presidential advisers in the U.S. government.

CARTRIDGE
The metal casing for a bullet.

CIVIL RIGHTS
The rights of citizens to be treated equally under the law.

COLONY
A region or country that is controlled by another more powerful country.

CONFEDERACY
The Southern states during the Civil War. Those supporting the Confederacy are known as Confederates.

CONGRESS
The legislative branch of the U.S. government, made up of the Senate and the House of Representatives.

CONSTITUTION
The body of laws that defines how a nation, such as the U.S., is governed.

DIXIE
Historical nickname for the states of the Confederacy.

FRIGATE
A type of warship built for speed and maneuverability.

GHETTO
A slum area of a city, often inhabited by a racial minority.

HANDCAR
A railroad vehicle powered by passengers, usually by moving a hand crank.

HYDROGEN
A flammable gas that is lighter than air, used to inflate balloons.

IRONCLAD
A warship protected by iron-plated armor.

LYNCHING
An illegal punishment, such as a hanging, carried out by an uncontrolled mob of people.

MEDAL OF HONOR
The U.S.A.'s highest military honor, awarded for acts of courage.

MERCHANT SHIP
A ship that transports cargo or paying passengers.

MILITIA
A group of armed civilians who are not professional soldiers.

MINISTER
Someone who holds a religious office, such as a preacher, or a politician in charge of a government department.

MUSKET
A type of gun that is loaded through the muzzle (shooting end).

PENICILLIN
A medicine taken to cure bacterial infections.

PLANTATION
A large farm or estate growing a particular crop, such as cotton.

RATIFY
To give legal approval for something, such as an election or an amendment to the Constitution.

RECONSTRUCTION
The policy of rebuilding the ruined southern states after the Civil War.

RESERVATION
An area of land inhabited by a Native American tribe.

RIFLING
The spiral grooves inside the barrel of the gun that make a bullet spin and therefore travel farther.

SECEDE
To break away, especially from a territorial political union.

SEGREGATION
A policy of keeping people of different races apart in public places.

TELEGRAPH
A system of electrical communication using a wire to send messages.

TORPEDO
In the Civil War, the word used to describe a floating mine (bomb).

UNION
A federation of states. In the Civil War, the name for the northern states.

INDEX

Picture credits (t=top, b=bottom, l=left, r=right, c=center, fc=front cover, bc=back cover)

All images are from the Library of Congress and the National Archive, except:
Dreamstime: bcb, 4bl Chris Minor, 4–5b John Bilous, 5tr Brandon Bourdages, 12–13b Americanspirit, 42–43b Mariusz Blach, 43cl Dani3315.
Wikimedia Commons: 10cr Daderot, 10br Bonnachoven, 32br Matthew Gordon, 66c Raphaël Thiémard, 71cl Sue Ream.